THE

MA

TIPS

MEG AVENT

THE LITTLE BOOK OF MACAROON TIPS

MEG AVENT

Absolute Press

First published in Great Britain in 2010 by
Absolute Press
Scarborough House, 29 James Street West
Bath BA1 2BT, England
Phone 44 (0) 1225 316013 **Fax** 44 (0) 1225 445836
E-mail info@absolutepress.co.uk
Web www.absolutepress.co.uk

A catalogue record of this book is available from the British Library

ISBN 13: 9781906650469

Printed and bound in Malta on behalf of Latitude Press

‘Blossom of the almond trees,
April’s gift to April’s bees.’

Sir Edwin Arnold,
English poet and journalist

1

When you have finished piping,

rap the tray a couple of times

on the edge of your work surface to get rid of any air bubbles.

2

Unless you have a willing helper,

use a jug or vase

to hold your piping bag open while you fill it.

3

After piping your uncooked macaroons

leave them to rest for 20–30 minutes

to form a skin and become dry to the touch. This will stop them cracking during baking.

4

Don’t pull the macaroons from the parchment paper.

If they won’t slide off easily, place them in the freezer for a few seconds or spray water between the parchment and the baking tray.

5

Too much filling can ruin the 'foot' of your macaroon

– just pipe a teaspoon full and twist the pair of shells together.

6

Store your filled macaroons in the fridge for 24 hours

before eating to allow the filling to melt slightly into the crisp shell. Let them come back to room temperature before serving.

7

For a small delectable

French-style macaroon,

pipe them 3cm in diameter, using a nozzle of 1cm.

8

Macaroons freeze very well,

so if you make a big batch you can freeze them for up to 6 weeks.

9

Filled shells are at their best after 3–4 days in the fridge.

Unfilled shells can be kept for up to 7 days.

10

To get consistent-sized macaroons

use a circle template to draw onto the reverse side of your paper – resist the urge to fill the full circle as the batter will spread.

11

Having trouble detaching your macaroons from the paper?

Use a silicone baking mat

and the shells will just pop off!

12

Liquid food colouring may destabilise egg whites –

it's best to use gel, paste or powder colouring.

13

Every oven is different and the recipe

temperature is always only a guide especially when it comes to delicate macaroons – sorry it's just a matter of trial and error!

14

Prepare ahead – **allow your egg whites to rise to room temperature** before you try and whip them – they will whip and hold better.

15

Humidity is a macaroon's worst enemy.

Don't even attempt to make them on wet or muggy days!

16

For small batches the French and Spanish methods are faster and easier –

for larger batches the Italian cooked meringue method works better.

17

For truly mouth-watering macaroons,

correspond your colouring to your flavouring

– think green for pistachio and lime, pink for raspberry – (you get the picture!).

18

If you are using parchment paper,

pipe a small dot of batter into each corner

of the baking tray – this will keep your paper in place while you pipe.

19

For big kids everywhere!

Fix brightly-coloured macaroons onto lolly sticks

and tie a ribbon around.

20

Fold your

dry ingredients

into your beaten egg whites

in 2–3
additions.

Adding them in one go could result in a too runny batter.

21

Always

use a toothpick to add gel or paste food colouring – a little really does go a long way!

22

Take extra care when making chocolate macaroons

– over mixing can result in too much oil being released from the cocoa and ruining your batter.

23

Egg whites should be placed in a scrupulously clean bowl

and beaten with a scrupulously clean whisk – just the hint of fat will prevent your whites being whipped to the correct consistency.

24

When using the Italian hot syrup method be extremely careful. When adding it to the egg whites

avoid getting any on the whisk

as splattering can cause burns.

25

Accurate measuring is paramount to achieving great results –

invest in digital scales!

26

When you take the macaroons out of the oven, put your baking trays onto a rack to cool before removing the paper.

If space is a problem use stacked wire racks.

27

Keep a watchful eye on the last few minutes of baking. To check if the macaroons are ready put a finger on one – it should be firm with the slightest amount of give –

if you feel a wobble give them a few more minutes.

28

For a less sweet filling

– try lemon curd or raspberry preserve.

29

If you are finding your oven is just too hot –

use two baking sheets

and lay a piece of parchment between them to insulate.

30

Sprinkle strawberry macaroons with black pepper

before you bake – it really does taste delicious.

31

To check batter consistency

– pick up a little with your finger – it should form a gentle peak that quickly dissolves back into the batter.

32

To make heart-shaped macaroons

pipe two overlapping circles – fill with Champagne whipped cream and serve as a Valentine gift.

33

Store your ground almonds in the freezer

to prevent them going rancid.

34

A little dried egg powder

can be added to tighten and stabilise the meringue and give it more holding time.

35

For a truly indulgent dessert:

add crushed macaroons

to lemon syllabub.

36

To check that your egg whites are beaten to the correct consistency

you should be able to invert the bowl

without the egg white falling out.

37

Use a tea strainer to sift cocoa or icing sugar on to your macaroons

for a simple but effective decoration.

38

If you see peaks after piping a whole row, **the mix is not ready.** Give it a few more turns.

39

Decorate your finished macaroons with edible glitter – especially beautiful –

gold hologram glitter on chocolate macaroons.

40

If your egg whites are very fresh

you can mimic the ageing process by placing them in the microwave on medium for 10 seconds – this should give a stronger meringue.

41

For a cute and pretty gift

– stack three macaroons in a clear cupcake box and tie with some silky satin ribbon.

42

When piping your batter

finish with a flick of the tip

upwards. This will help ensure a flat macaroon.

43

Never add oil-based colour

as it will destabilise your egg whites.

44

‘Age’ your egg whites

in the fridge for 24–48 hours before using; they will become stronger and hold their shape better when whipped.

45

For a beautiful personalised wedding favour, decorate your macaroon by

painting the happy couple's initials in edible gold paint onto the baked surface.

46

Don't over-mix your batter;

you will have trouble controlling the flow when piping.

47

For a macaroon that not only looks sensational but also smells divine – **fill dark pink ones with rose butter cream… mmm!**

48

For a subtle marble effect

– don't mix your food colouring completely.

49

Some shop-bought ground almonds can be a little course – **blitz in a food processor for a minute** to get them really fine.

50

Don’t despair!

Even if your macaroons don’t look perfect they will still taste delicious.

Meg Avent

Through her work in cookery book publishing, Meg has commissioned some of the country's leading patisserie chefs. Inspired by their work, and having always had a passion for cake decorating, she went on to train at one of London's leading cake companies. She now runs her own business, Lemon Sky Cakes, specialising in unique and beautiful wedding and celebration cakes.

www.lemonskycakes.co.uk

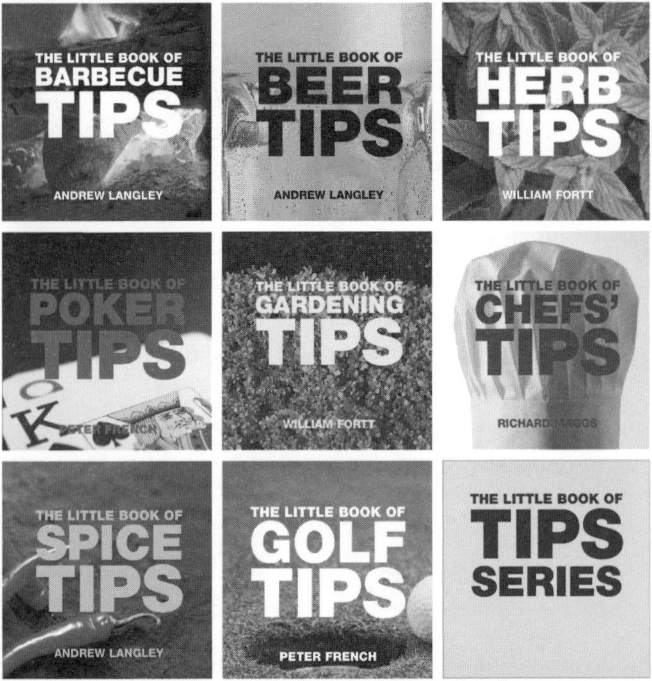
THE LITTLE BOOK OF BARBECUE TIPS
ANDREW LANGLEY
THE LITTLE BOOK OF BEER TIPS
ANDREW LANGLEY
THE LITTLE BOOK OF HERB TIPS
WILLIAM FORTT
THE LITTLE BOOK OF POKER TIPS
PETER FRENCH
THE LITTLE BOOK OF GARDENING TIPS
WILLIAM FORTT
THE LITTLE BOOK OF CHEFS' TIPS
RICHARD MAGGS
THE LITTLE BOOK OF SPICE TIPS
ANDREW LANGLEY
THE LITTLE BOOK OF GOLF TIPS
PETER FRENCH
THE LITTLE BOOK OF TIPS SERIES

THE LITTLE BOOK OF
CHEESE
TIPS
ANDREW LANGLEY

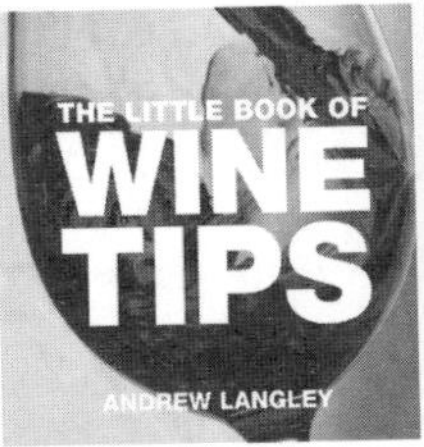
THE LITTLE BOOK OF
WINE
TIPS
ANDREW LANGLEY

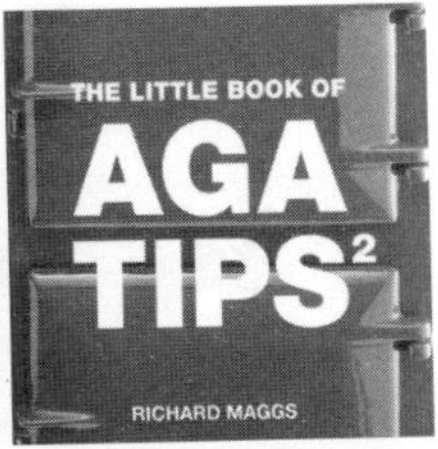
THE LITTLE BOOK OF
AGA
TIPS²
RICHARD MAGGS

THE LITTLE BOOK OF
COFFEE
TIPS
ANDREW LANGLEY

THE LITTLE BOOK OF
TEA
TIPS
ANDREW LANGLEY

THE LITTLE BOOK OF
AGA
TIPS³
RICHARD MAGGS

THE LITTLE BOOK OF
AGA
TIPS
RICHARD MAGGS

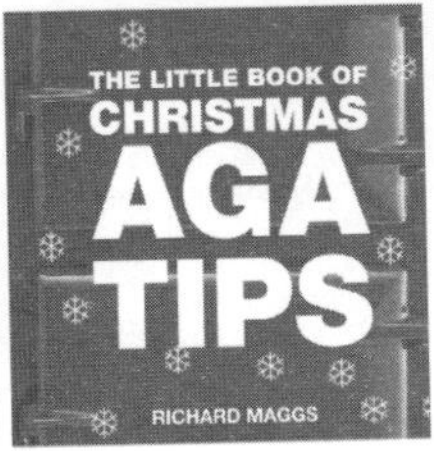
THE LITTLE BOOK OF
CHRISTMAS
AGA
TIPS
RICHARD MAGGS

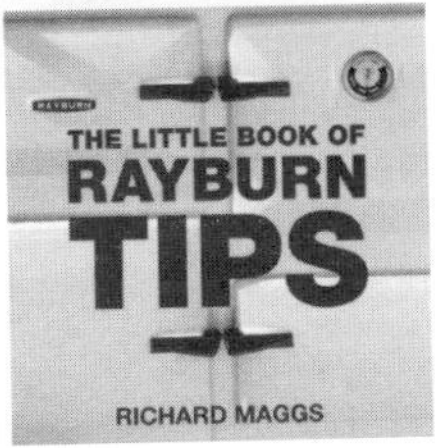
RAYBURN
THE LITTLE BOOK OF
RAYBURN
TIPS
RICHARD MAGGS

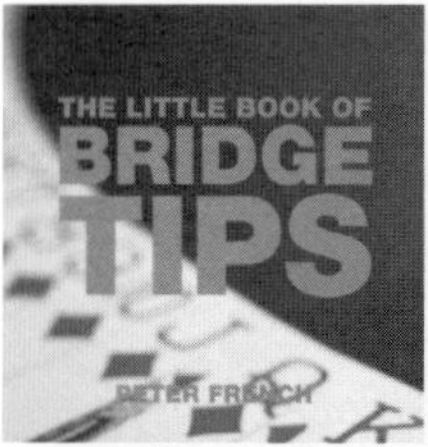
THE LITTLE BOOK OF
BRIDGE
TIPS
PETER FRENCH

THE LITTLE BOOK OF
CHESS
TIPS
PETER FRENCH

THE LITTLE BOOK OF
FISHING
TIPS
MICK DEVENISH

THE LITTLE BOOK OF
GREEN
TIPS
WILLIAM FORTT
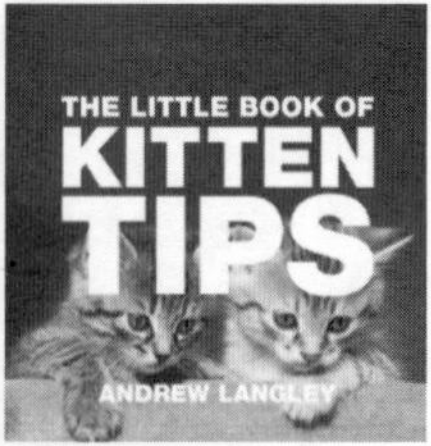
THE LITTLE BOOK OF
KITTEN
TIPS
ANDREW LANGLEY

MARMITE
PAUL HARTLEY
THE LITTLE BOOK OF
MARMITE
TIPS

THE LITTLE BOOK OF
PUPPY
TIPS
ANDREW LANGLEY

THE LITTLE BOOK OF
WHISKY
TIPS
ANDREW LANGLEY

THE LITTLE BOOK OF
TRAVEL
TIPS
MEGAN DEVENISH